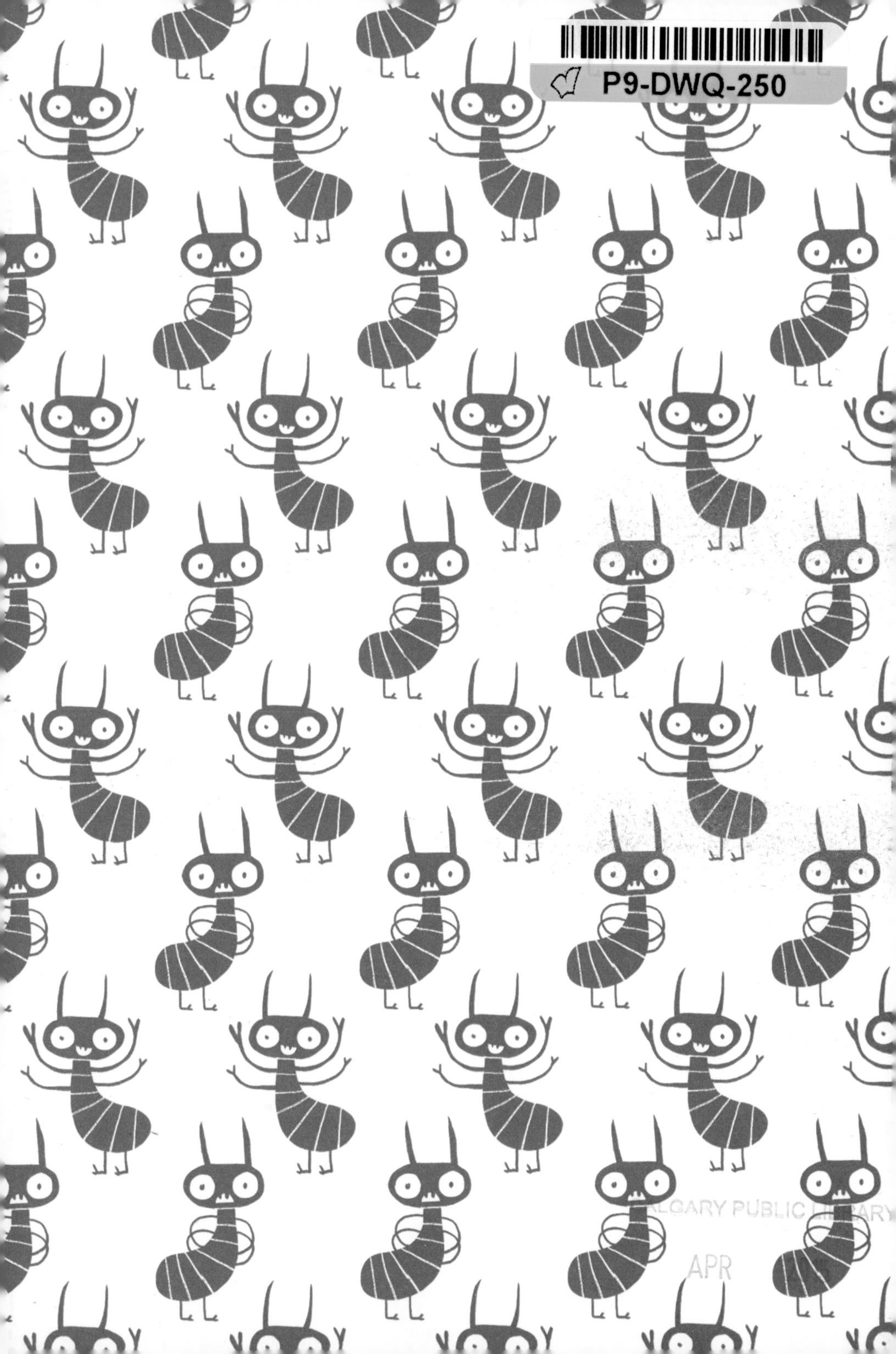

HEAD LICE

For Elie:
May your head be always free of lice

Originally published as *Le pou* by Les éditions de la courte échelle inc.

Copyright © 2015 Elise Gravel
Copyright for the French edition: Elise Gravel and Les éditions de la courte échelle inc., 2014

Published in Canada by Tundra Books, a division of Random House of Canada Limited,
One Toronto Street, Suite 300, Toronto, Ontario M5C 2V6

Published in the United States by Tundra Books of Northern New York,
P.O. Box 1030, Plattsburgh, New York 12901

Library of Congress Control Number: 2014941833

Library and Archives Canada Cataloguing in Publication

Gravel, Elise
[Pou. English]
    Head lice / written and illustrated by Élise Gravel.

(Disgusting critters)
Translation of: Le pou.
Issued in print and electronic formats.
ISBN 978-1-77049-661-3 (bound).—ISBN 978-1-77049-663-7 (epub)

    I. Lice—Juvenile literature. 2. Pediculosis—Juvenile literature. I. Title. II. Title: Pou. English.

QL540.G7213 2015   j595.7'56   C2014-903052-5
                                         C2014-903053-3

English edition edited by Samantha Swenson
Designed by Elise Gravel and Tundra Books
The artwork in this book was rendered digitally.

www.tundrabooks.com

Printed and bound in China

1 2 3 4 5 6   20 19 18 17 16 15

Elise Gravel

HEAD LICE

HEY THERE!

Tundra Books

A single head lice is called

A LOUSE.

Ladies and gentlemen, meet your new
louse friend!

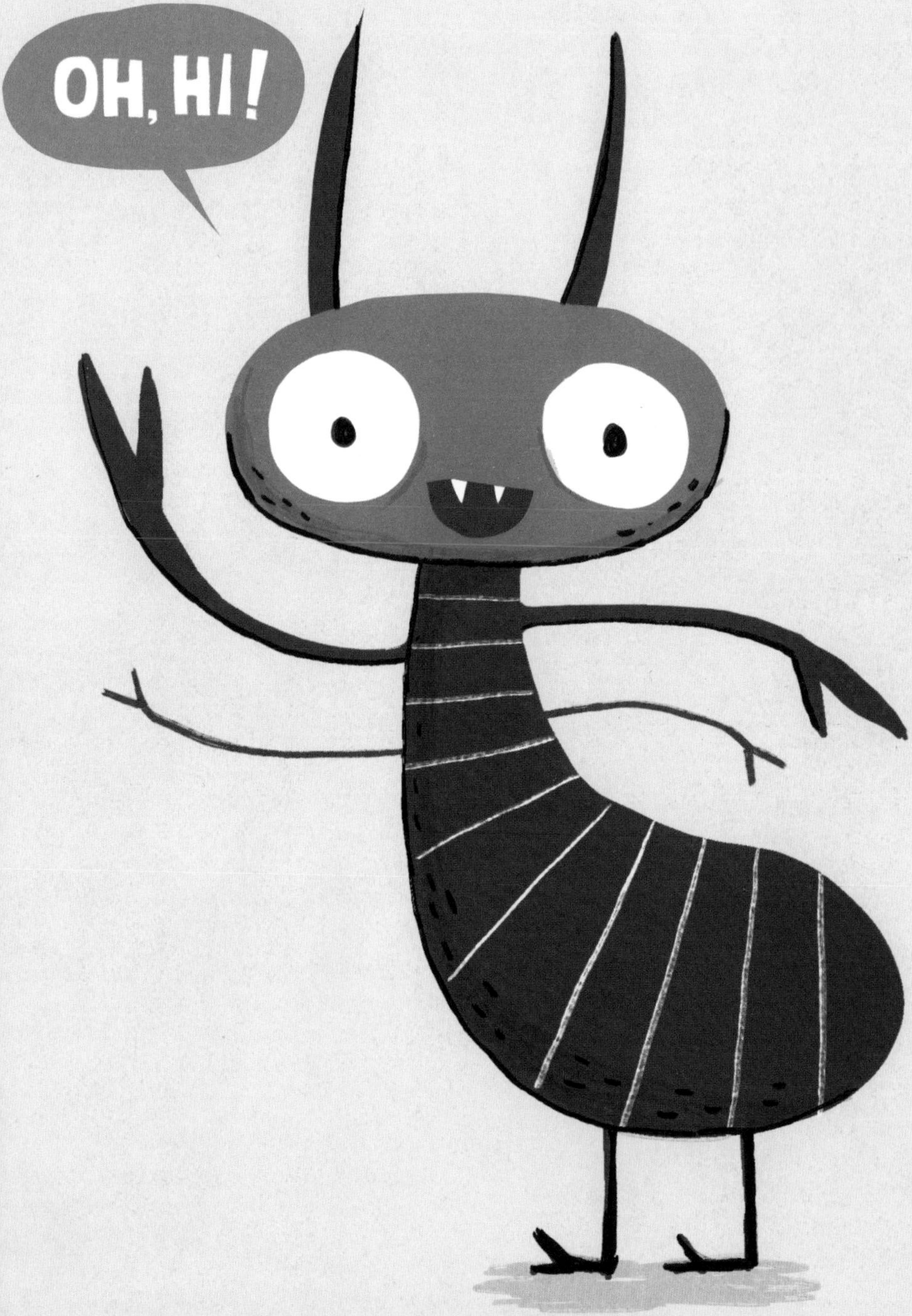
OH, HI!

The head louse has

SIX LEGS,

which makes him an

Well, it's pretty obvious I'm not a FRUIT!

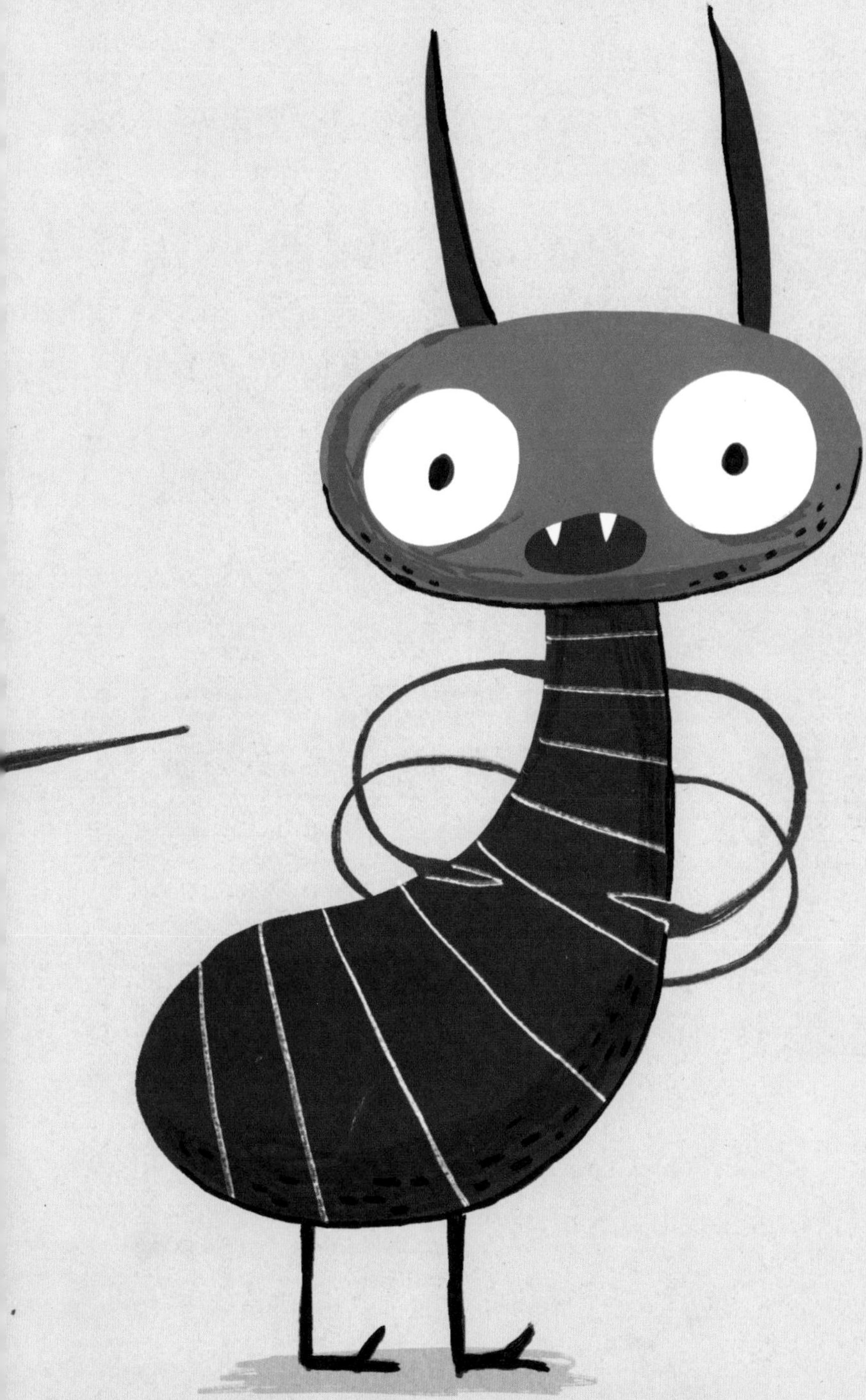

The head louse is about two and a half to three millimeters long, or an eighth of an inch. He's about the size of a

SESAME SEED.

I might be small, but to your parents, I'm scarier than a lion.

LOUSE

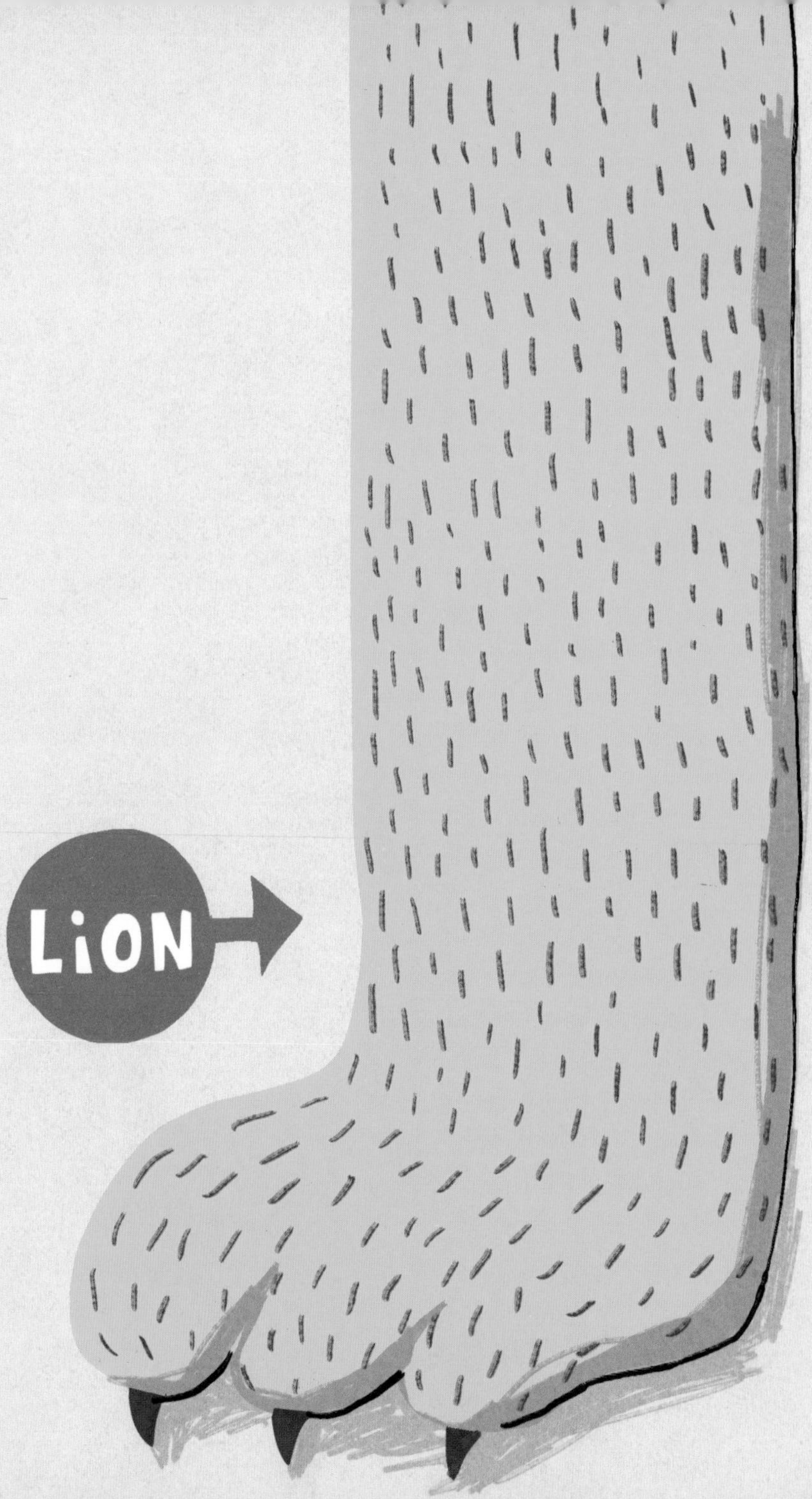
LiON

The head louse's body is slightly

TRANSPARENT,

so we can see inside his

TUMMY.

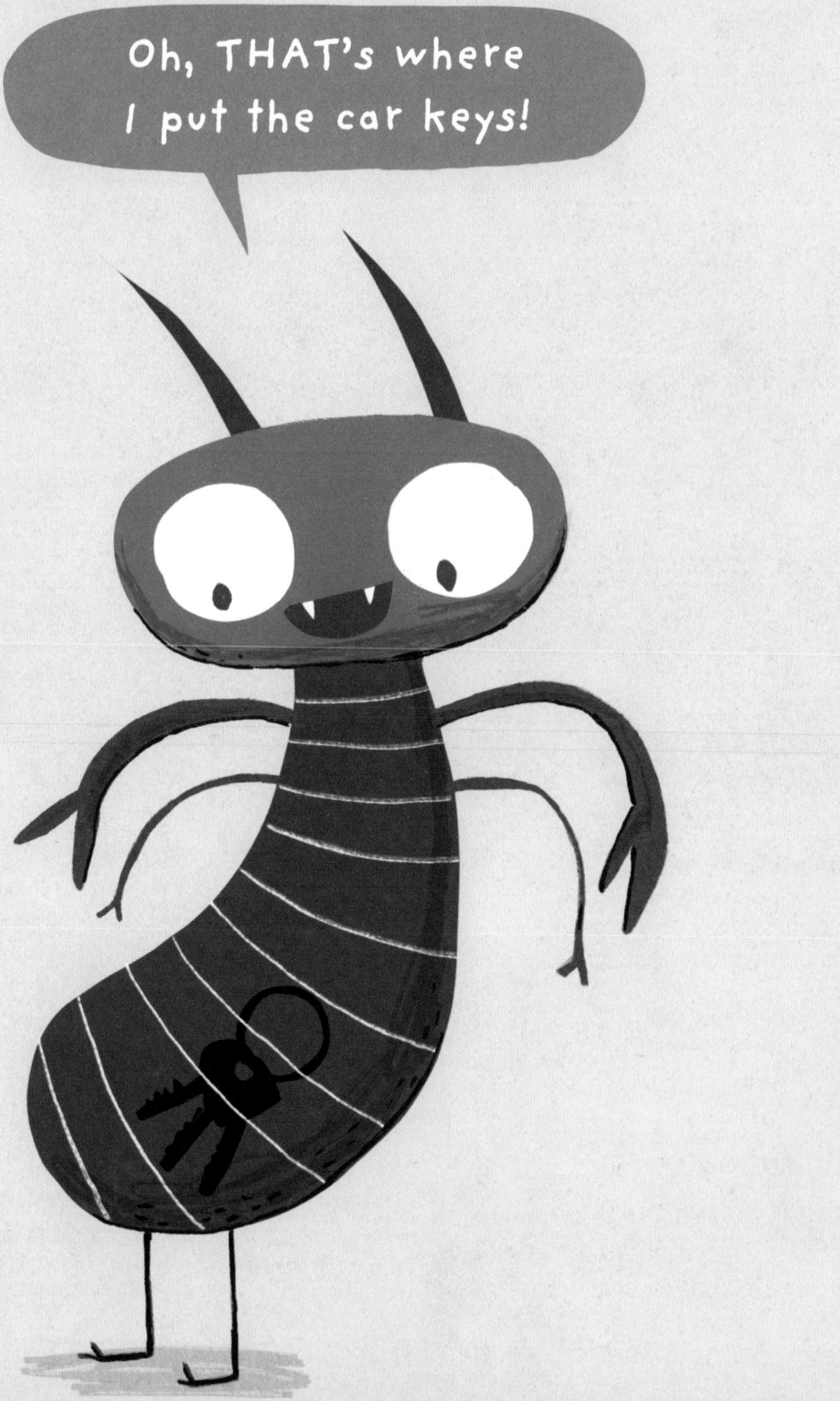
Oh, THAT's where I put the car keys!

He can't fly or jump, and because of his very

SHORT LEGS,

he even has trouble walking on flat surfaces.

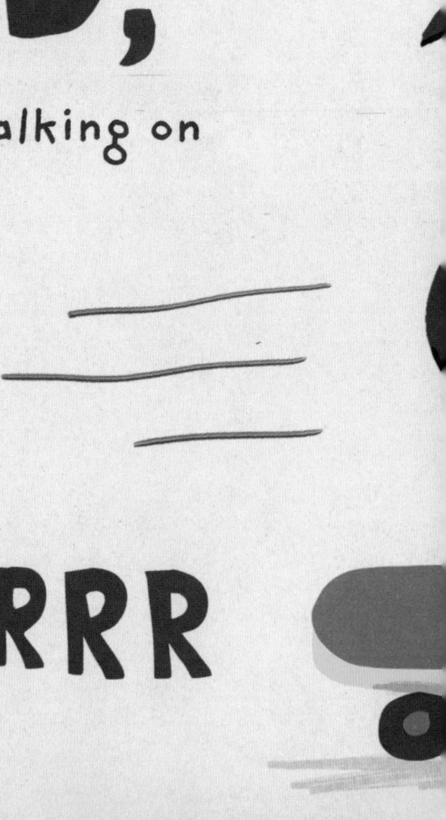

RRRRRRRRR

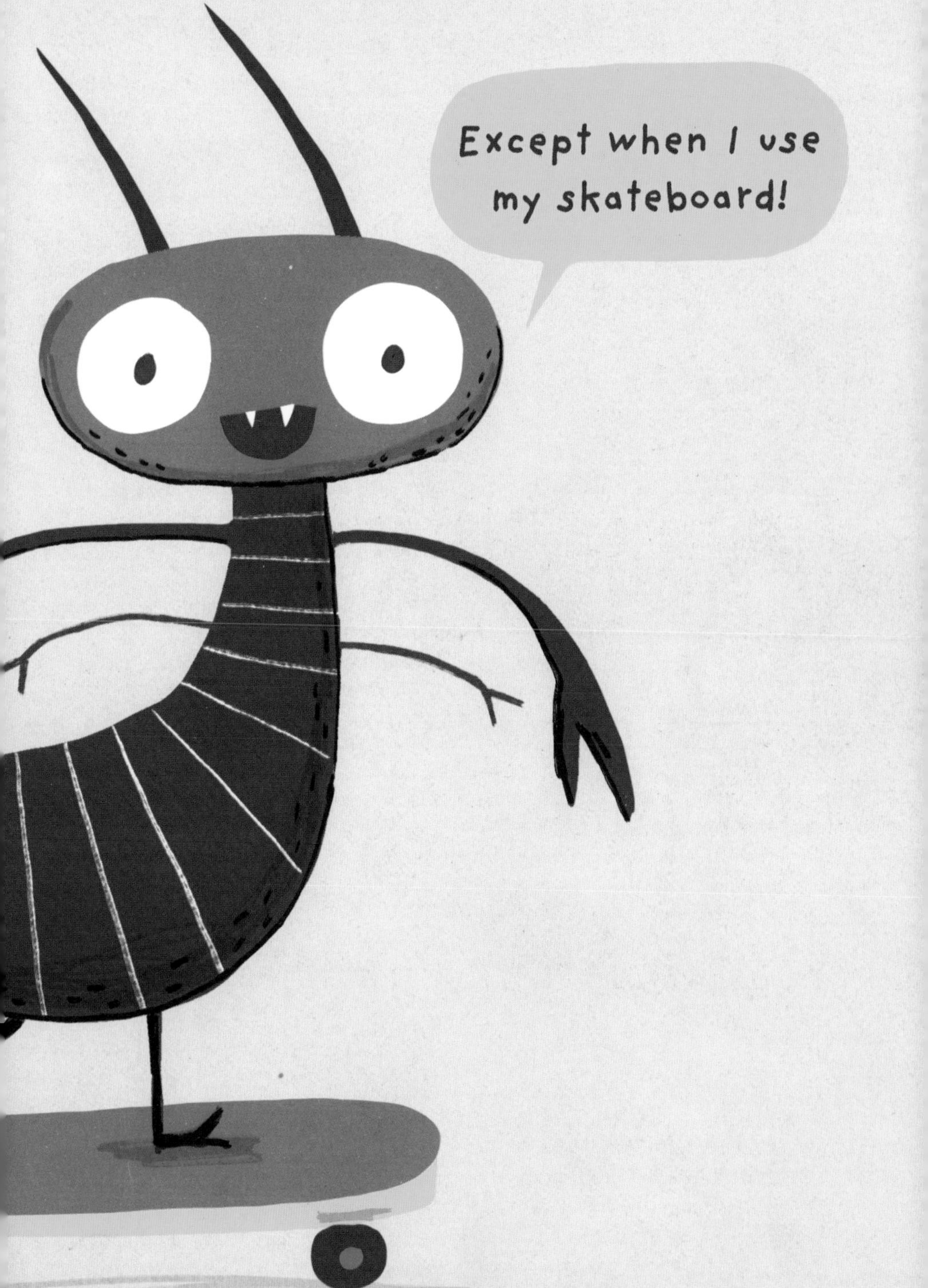
Except when I use
my skateboard!

With the use of a big thumb and

CLAW

at the end of his two front legs, he's very good at moving up and down hair and swinging from

ONE HAIR

to another.

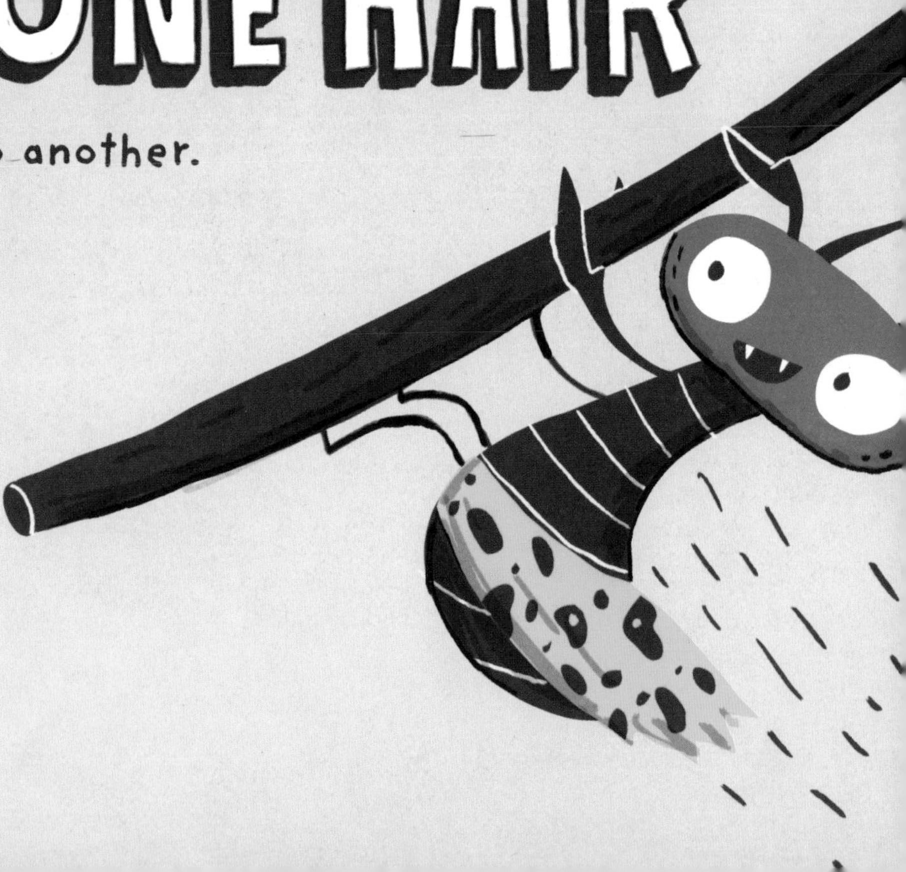

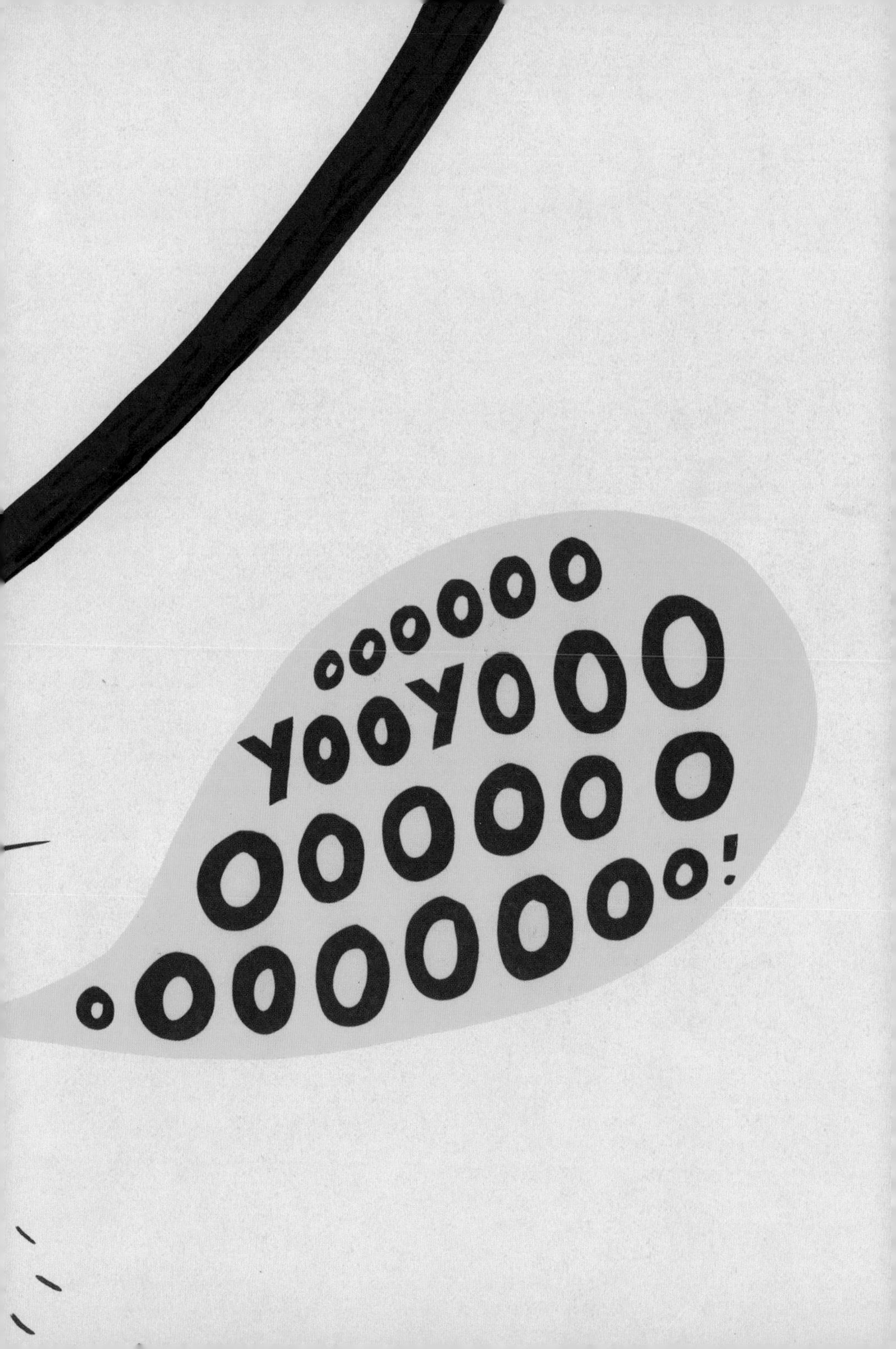
oooooo
YOOYOOO
OOOOOO
oOOOOOOo!

The louse is born, grows up and dies on a

HUMAN

head, and he lives for only 20 to 30 days. He can't live on any other animal or in any other environment.

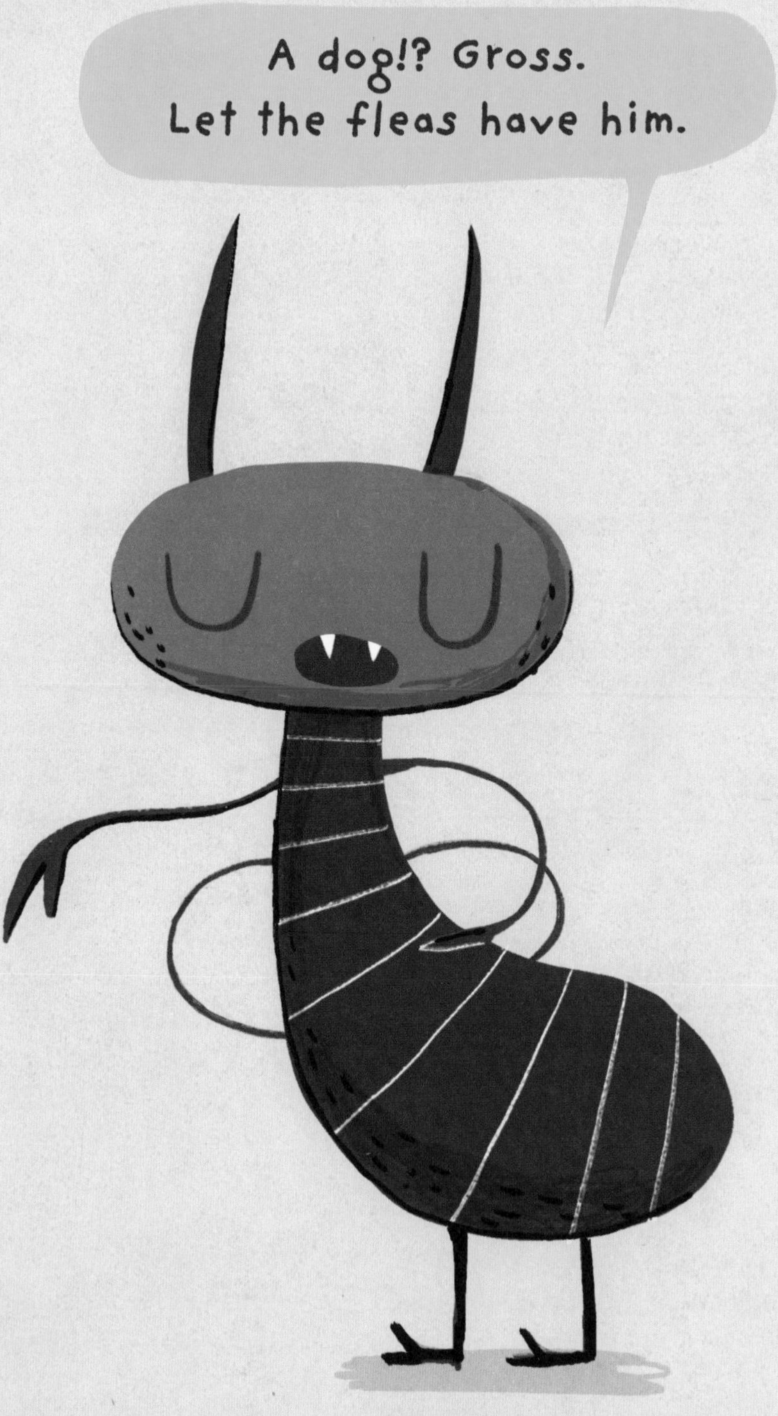
A dog!? Gross.
Let the fleas have him.

The louse's only food is

HUMAN BLOOD.

He drinks it about five times a day.

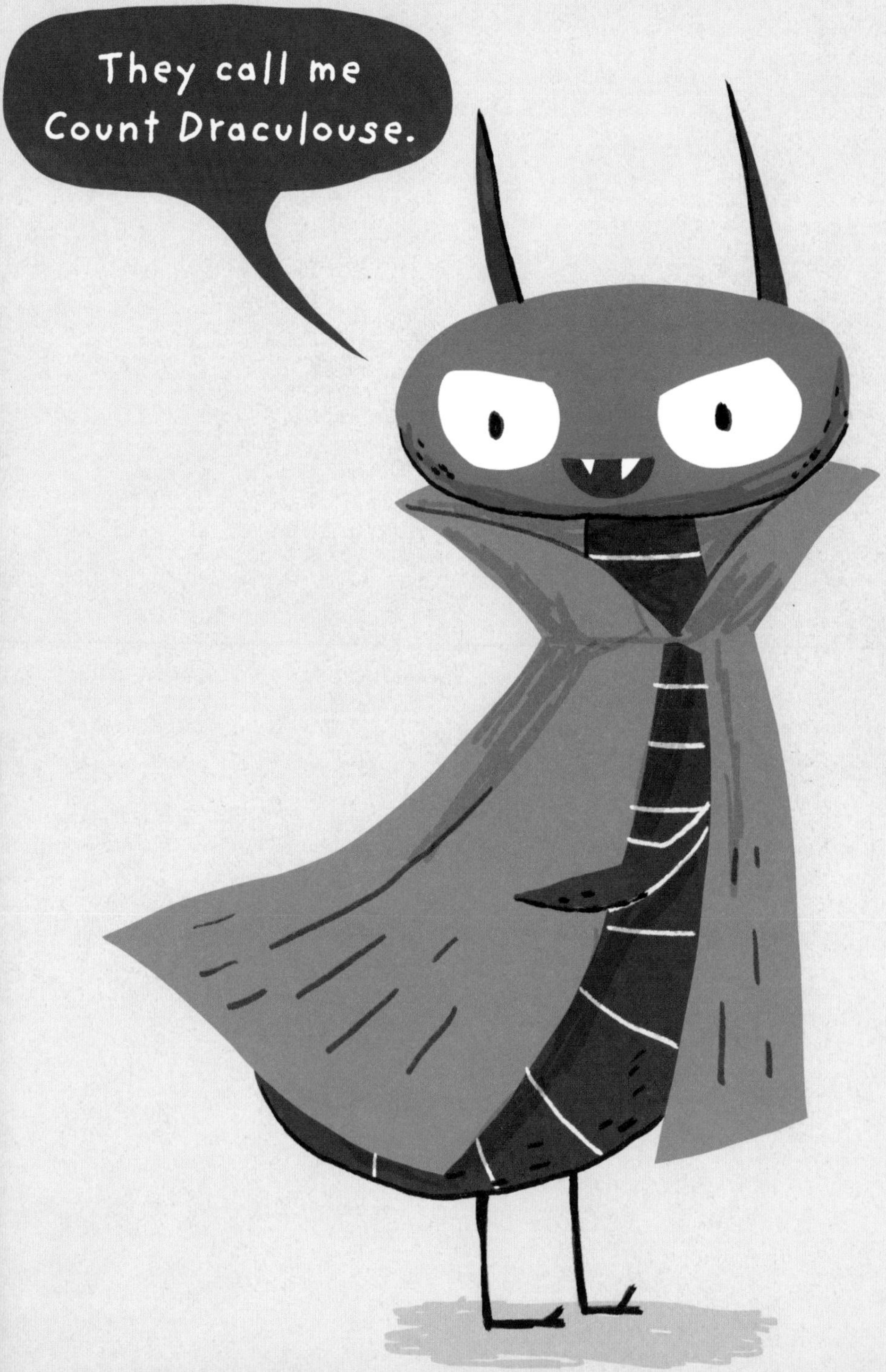
They call me Count Draculouse.

The female louse lays three to five eggs a day. The eggs are called

NITS.

She attaches them to the hair with a very sticky, gluelike substance she makes that hardens like cement.

I also use it to build my model airplanes!

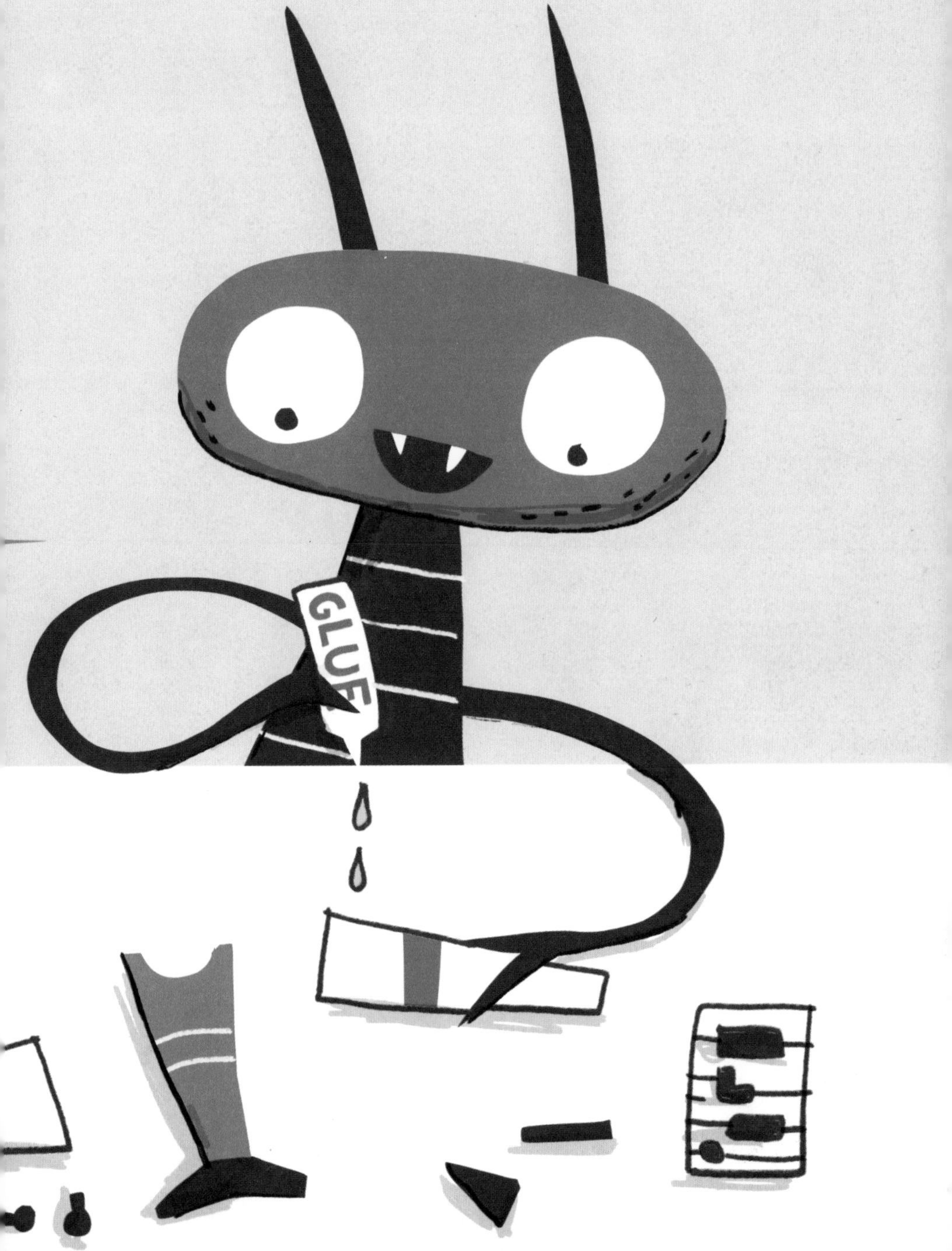
GLUE

The eggs stay stuck to the hair for seven to twelve days before they hatch. The young head lice, called

NYMPHS,

will soon reproduce too. If you don't get rid of them, you'll end up with a head full of lice!

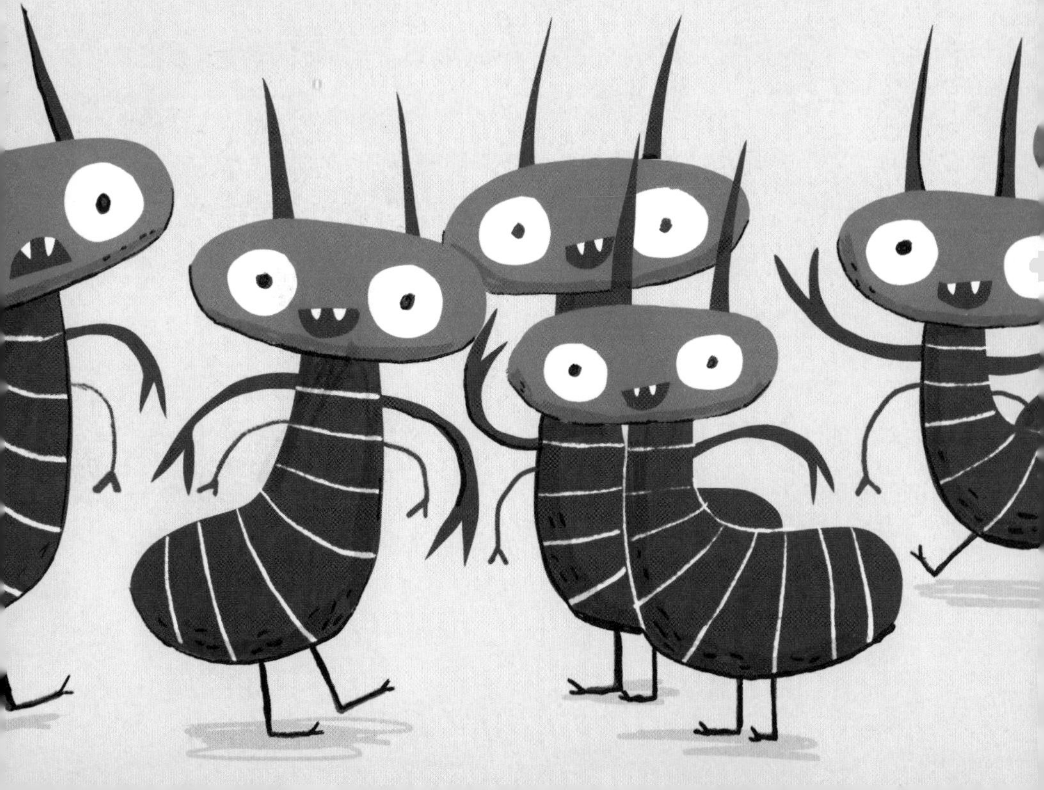

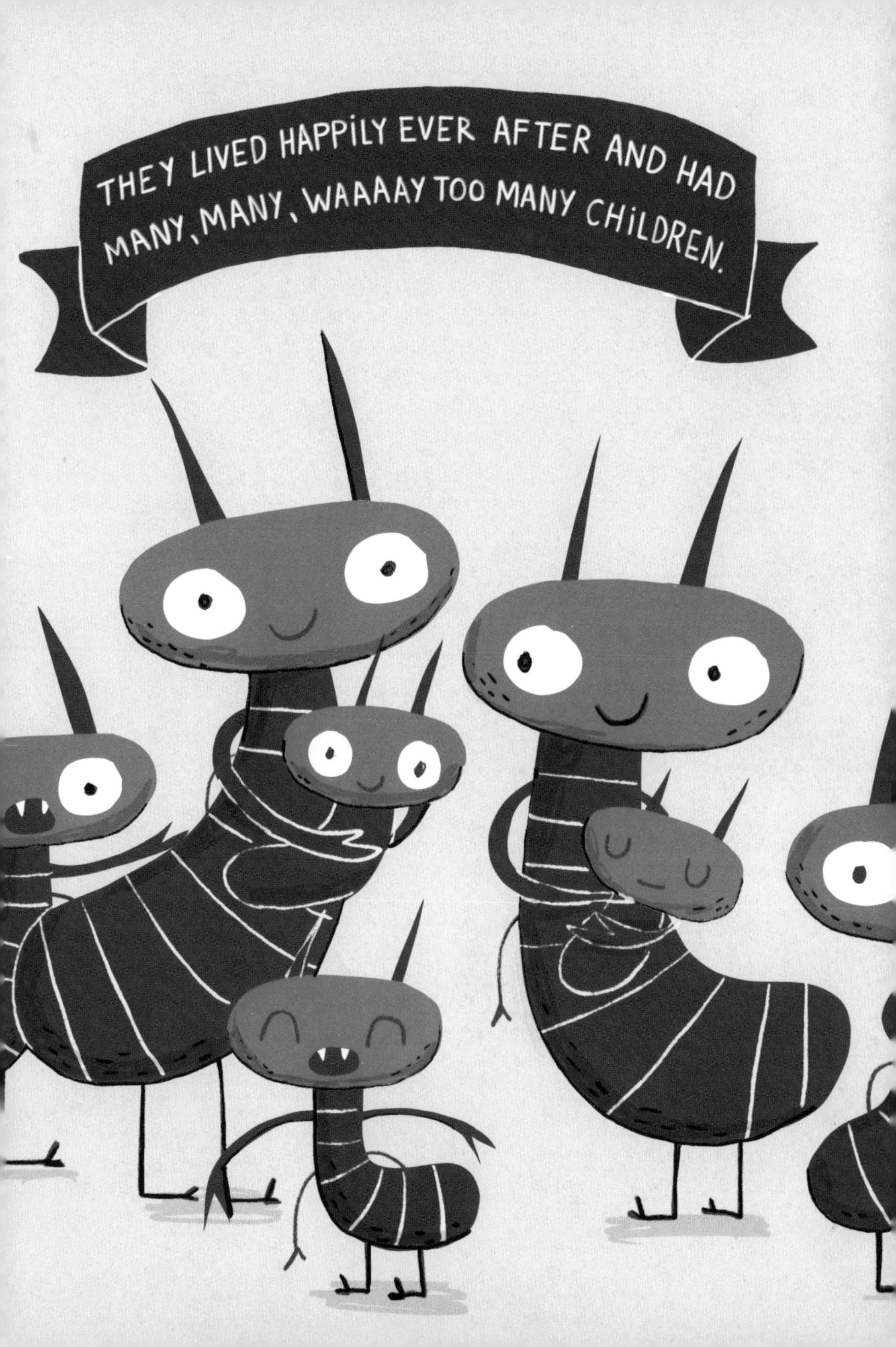
THEY LIVED HAPPILY EVER AFTER AND HAD MANY, MANY, WAAAAY TOO MANY CHILDREN.

To go from one head to another, the louse has to wait for

HEADS

to touch or for people to exchange hats or clothes with lice on them. He doesn't care one bit if you're clean or dirty!

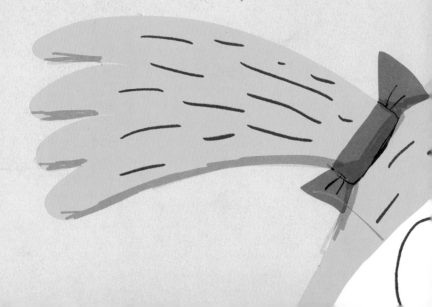

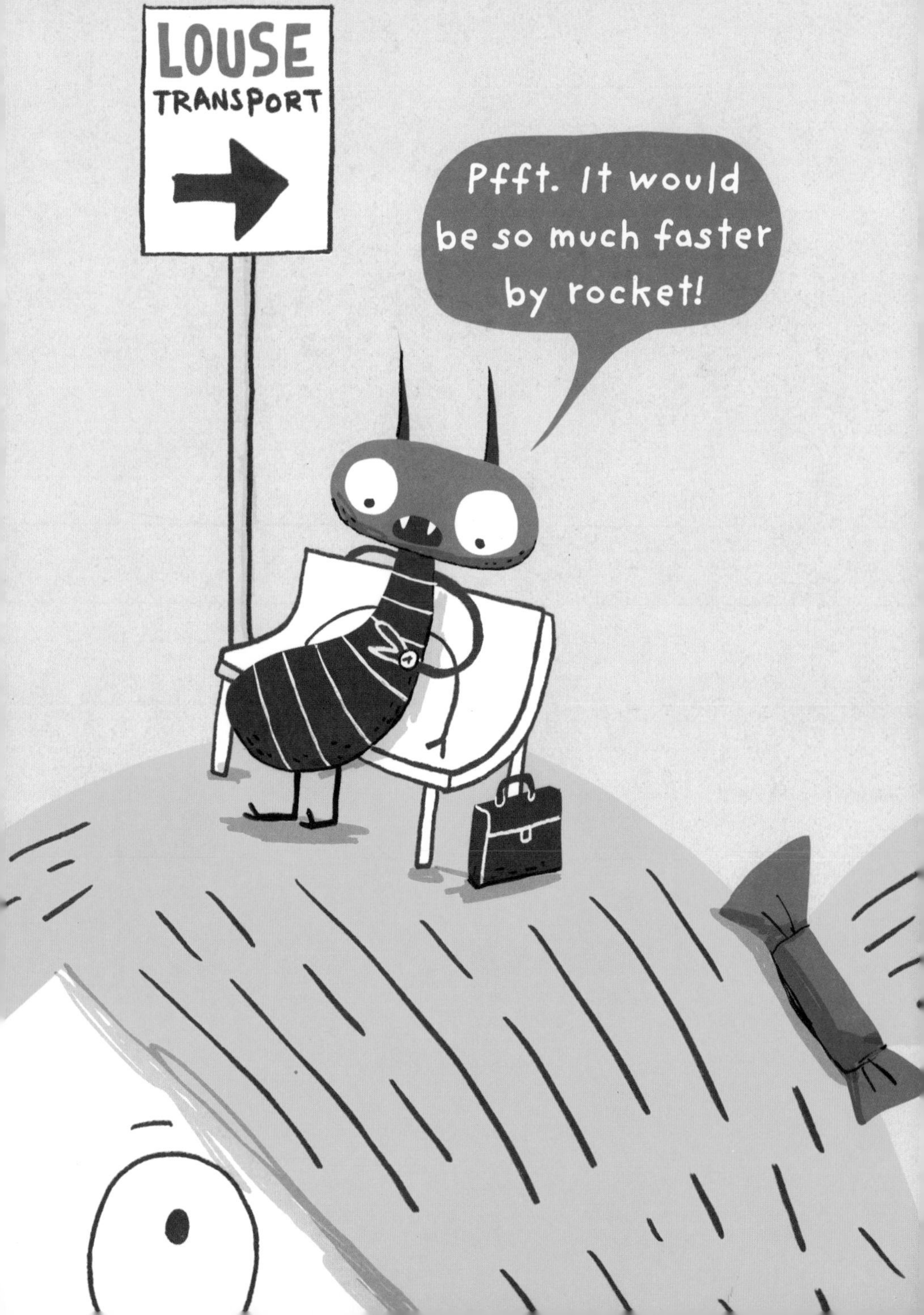
LOUSE
TRANSPORT
Pfft. It would be so much faster by rocket!

The head louse might be

GROSS AND ANNOYING

and give you some itchy bites, but he's not dangerous.

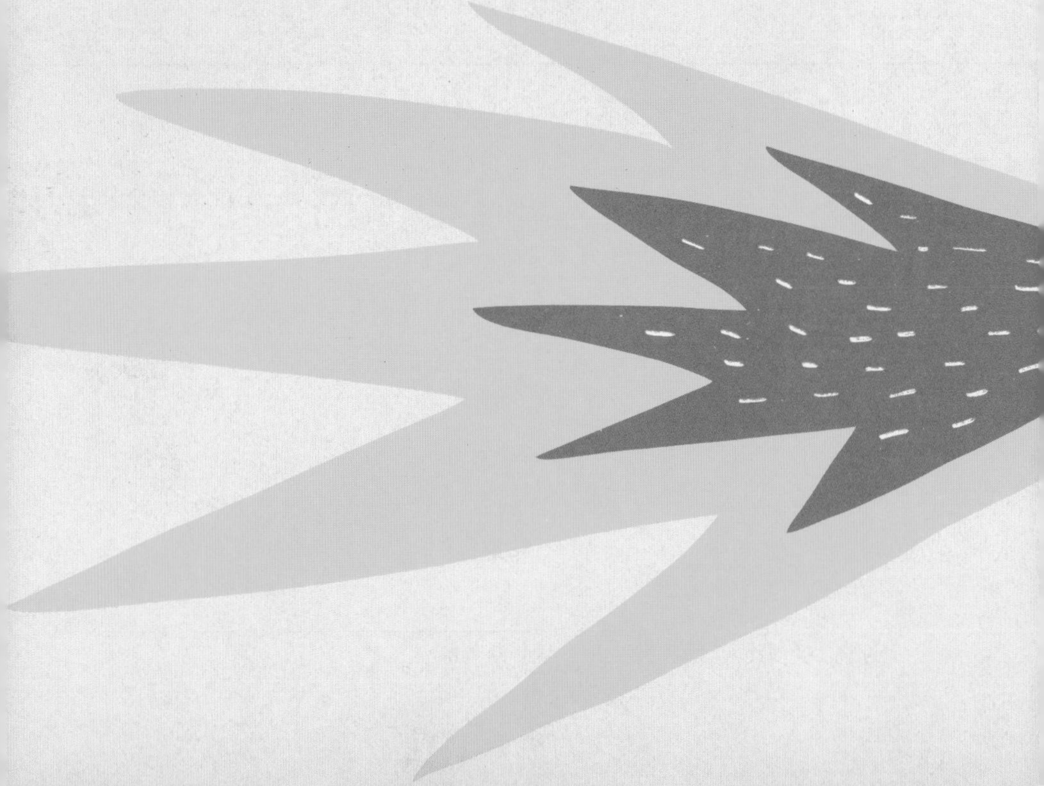

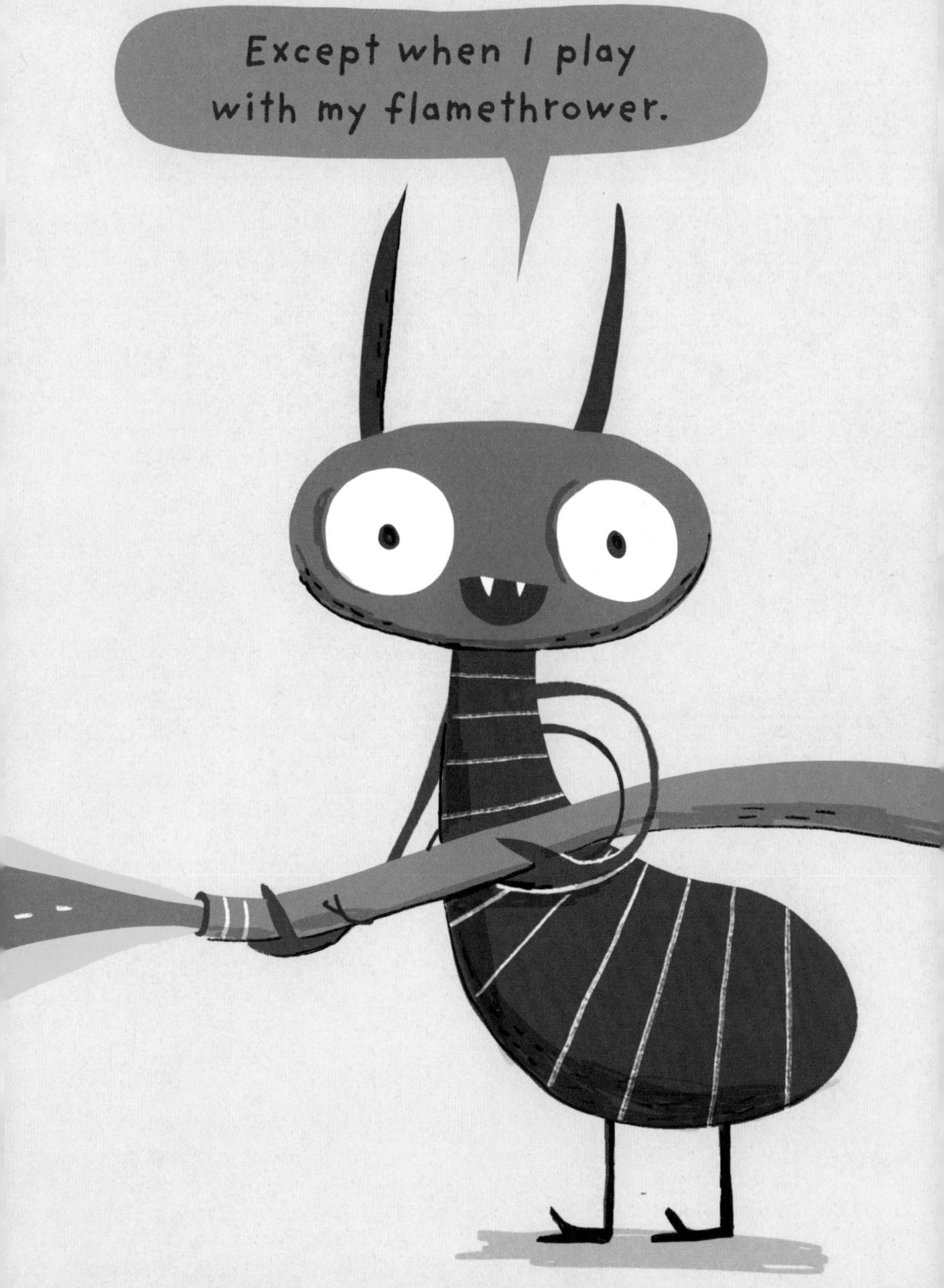
Except when I play with my flamethrower.

The head louse is really useful for . . . hmm . . . uh . . . well,

NOTHING AT ALL,

really!

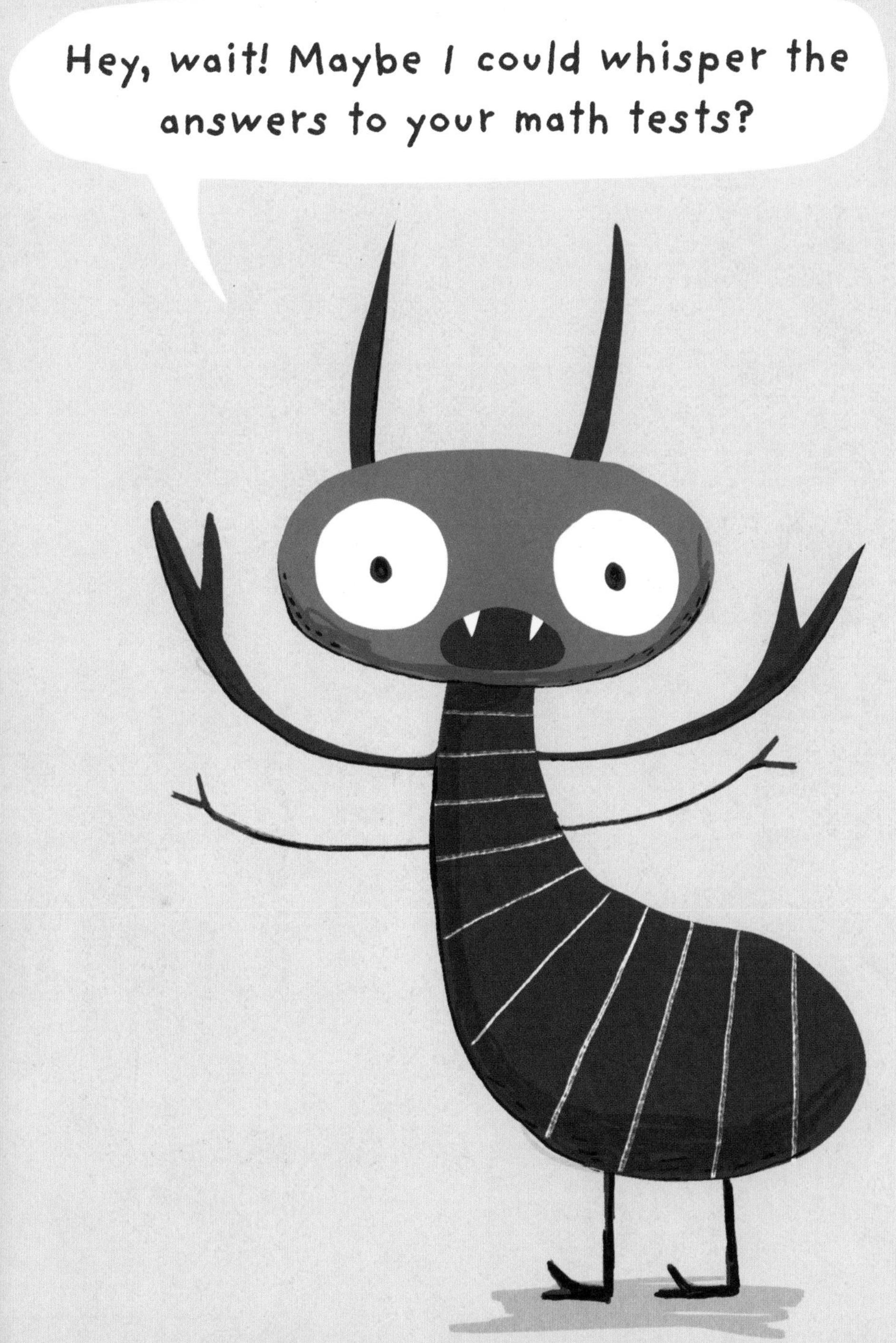
Hey, wait! Maybe I could whisper the answers to your math tests?

So the next time you see a head louse . . .

RUN AWAY!

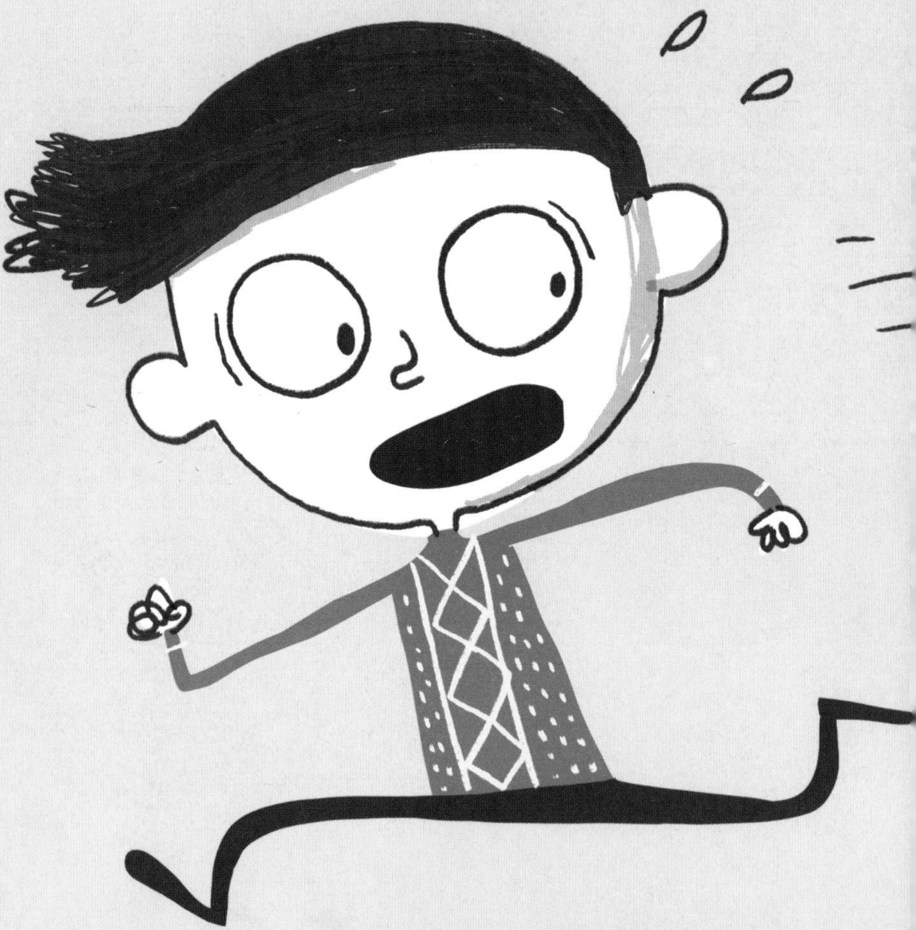

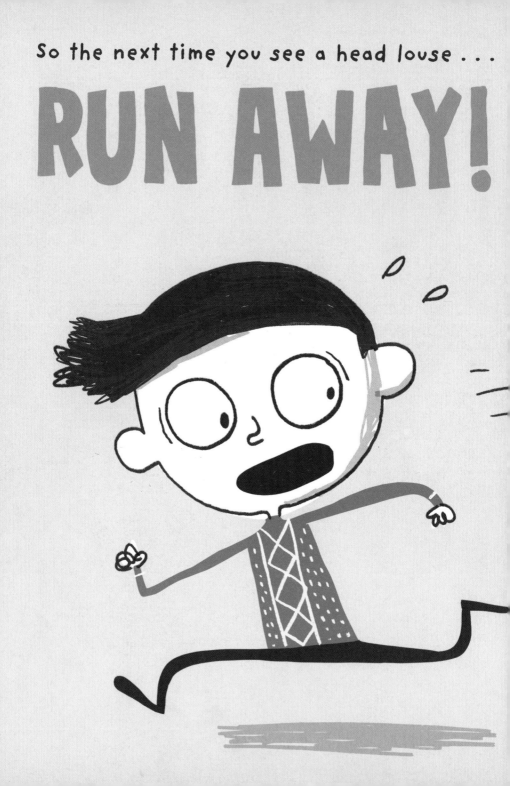

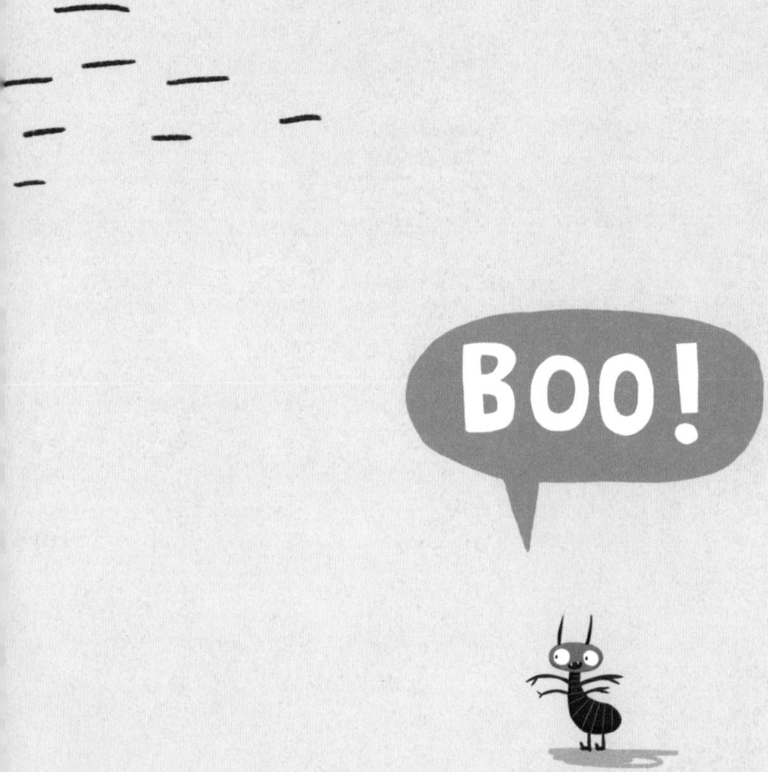
BOO!

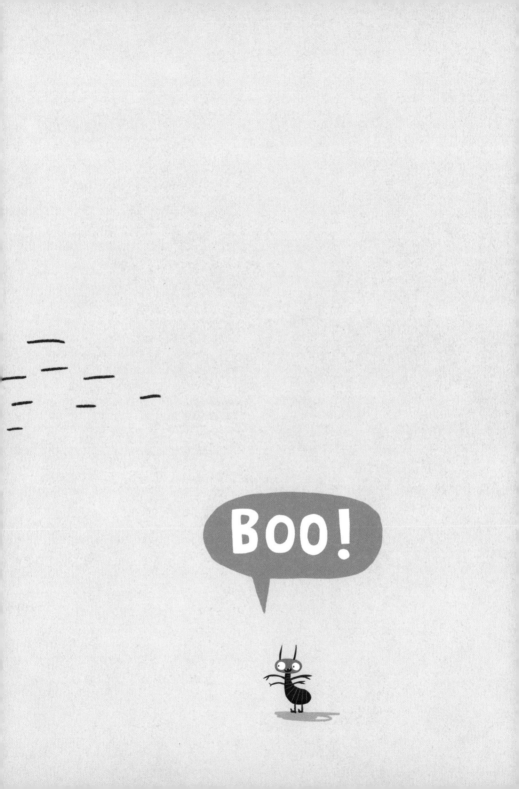

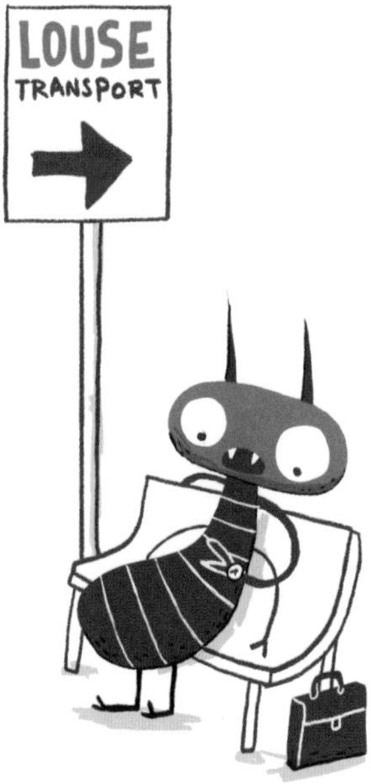
LOUSE
TRANSPORT

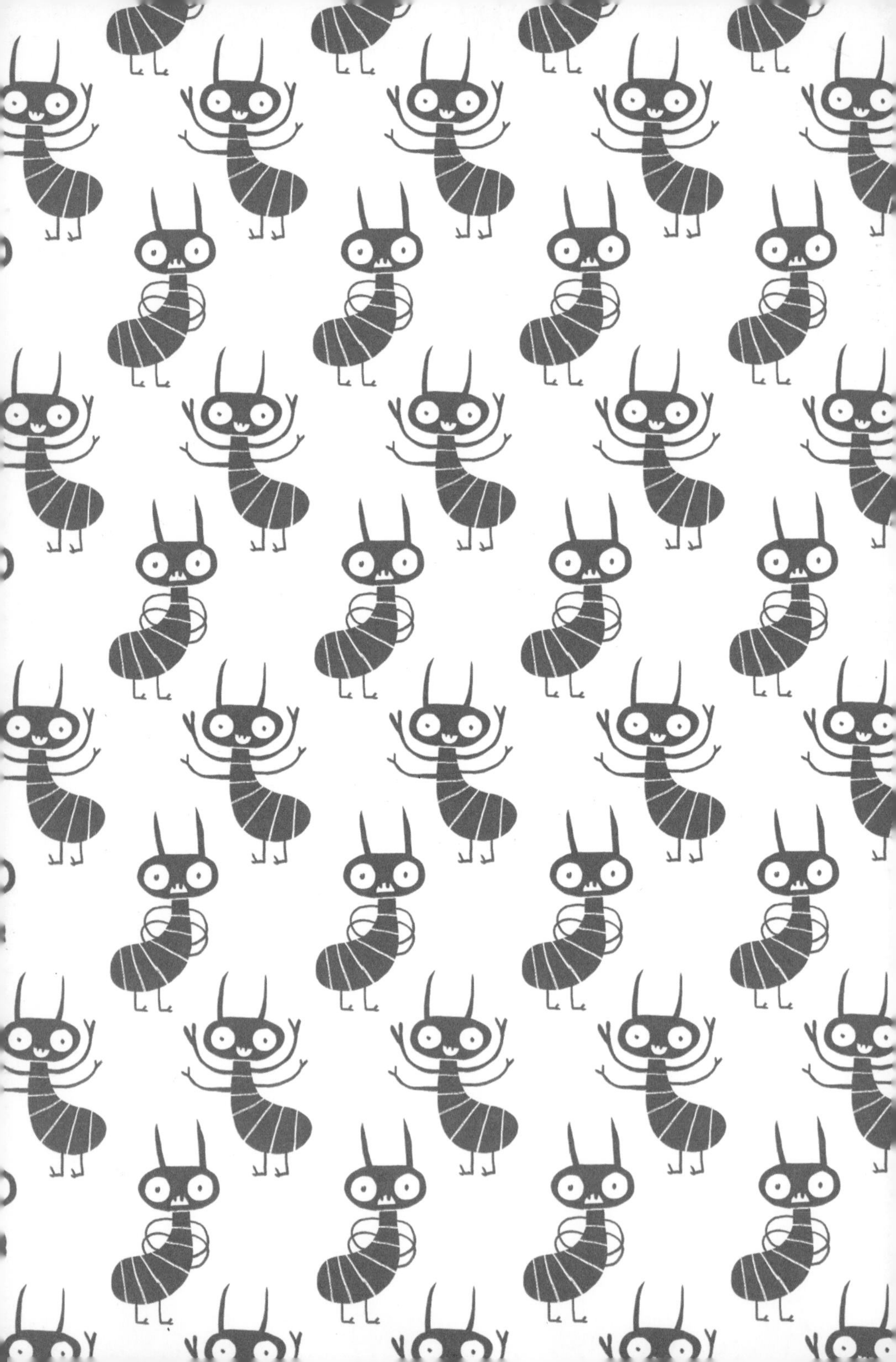